Chord Bassics

By Jonas Hellborg.

Exclusive Distributors:
Music Sales Limited
8/9 Frith Street, London W1V 5TZ, England
Music Sales Corporation
24 East 22nd Street, New York, N.Y. 10010, USA
Music Sales Pty. Limited
27 Clarendon Street, Artarmon, Sydney, NSW 2064, Australia

© Copyright Day Eight Music Production, Sweden.
This edition © Copyright 1986 by Amsco Publications
UK ISBN 0.7119.0717.X
US ISBN 0.8256.1058.3
Order No. AM 60138

Cover design by Alison Fenton (UK)

Music Sales complete catalogue lists thousands of
titles and is free from your local music book shop,
or direct from Music Sales Limited.
Please send 50p in stamps for postage to
Music Sales Limited, 8/9 Frith Street, London W1V 5TZ.

Printed in England by Printwise (Haverhill) Limited

Amsco Publications
New York/London/Sydney/Cologne

EXPLANATION OF SYMBOLS

CHORD SYMBOLS

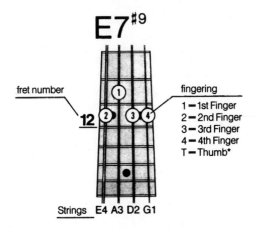

fret number

12

fingering

1 — 1st Finger
2 — 2nd Finger
3 — 3rd Finger
4 — 4th Finger
T — Thumb*

Strings   E4 A3 D2 G1

*   After picking or strumming the stopped strings the thumb is 'hammered' on the fret shown to complete the chord.

C	— C major
C△7	— C major seventh
C△7#11	— C major seventh sharp eleven
C 6/9	— C sixth ninth
C 6	— C sixth
C7	— C seventh
C7 sus 4	— C seventh sus four
C9	— C ninth
C11	— C eleventh
C13	— C thirteenth
C7♭9	— C seventh flat nine
C7#9	— C seventh sharp nine
C7♭5	— C seventh flat five
C7#5	— C seventh sharp five
C-	— C minor
C-6	— C minor sixth
C-♭6	— C minor flat sixth
C-7	— C minor seventh
C-9	— C minor ninth
C-7♭5	— C minor seventh flat five
C°	— C diminished

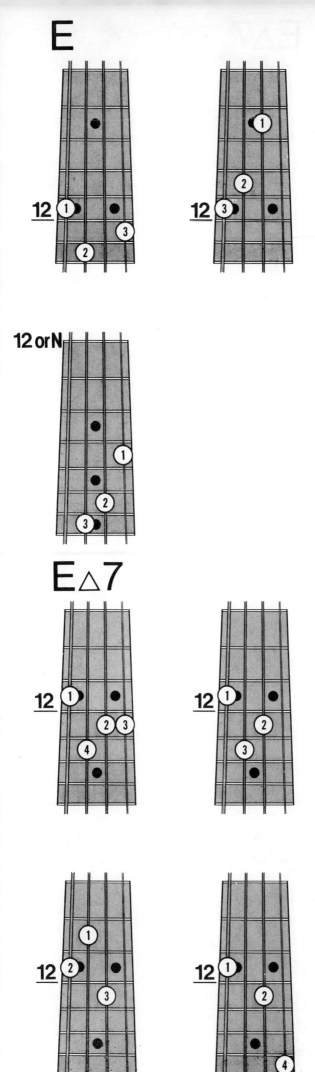

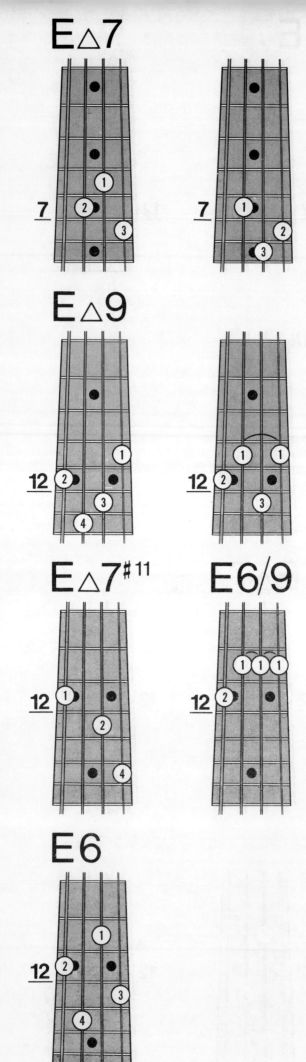

6

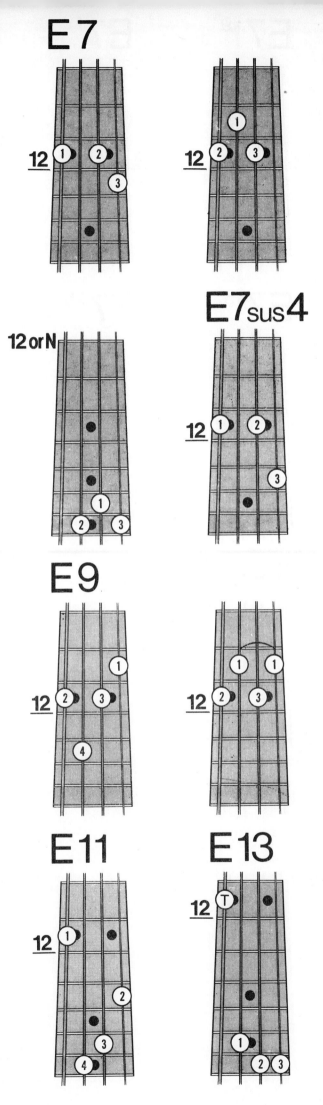

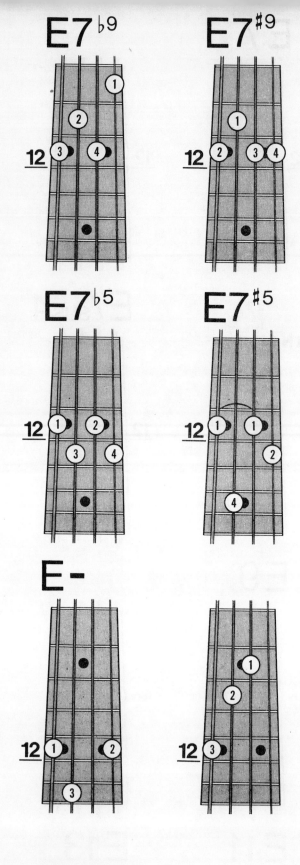

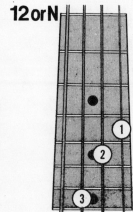

E-6

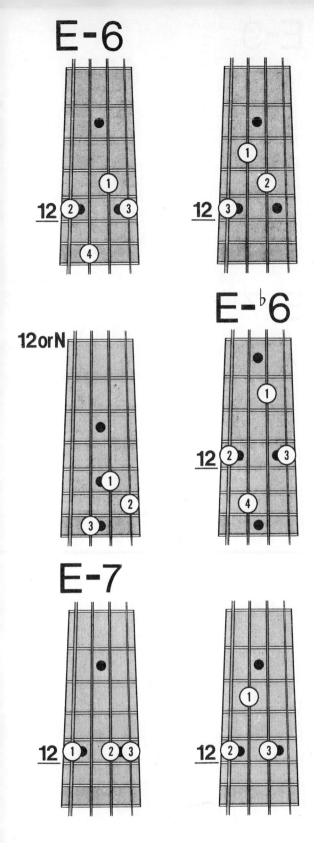

E-♭6

E-7

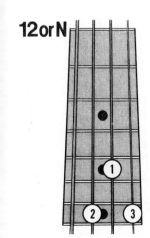

9

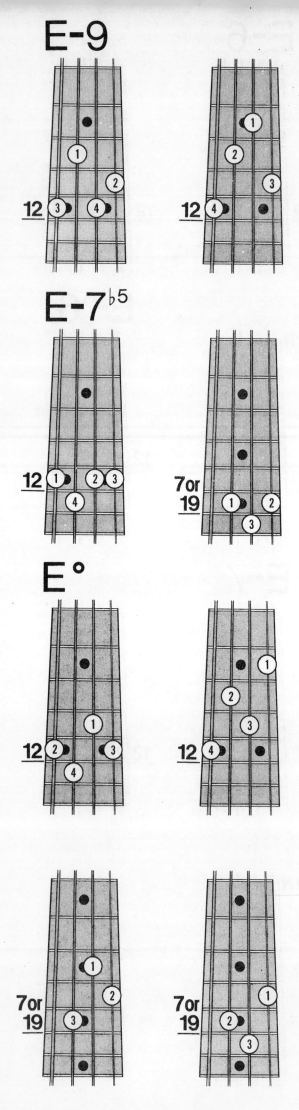

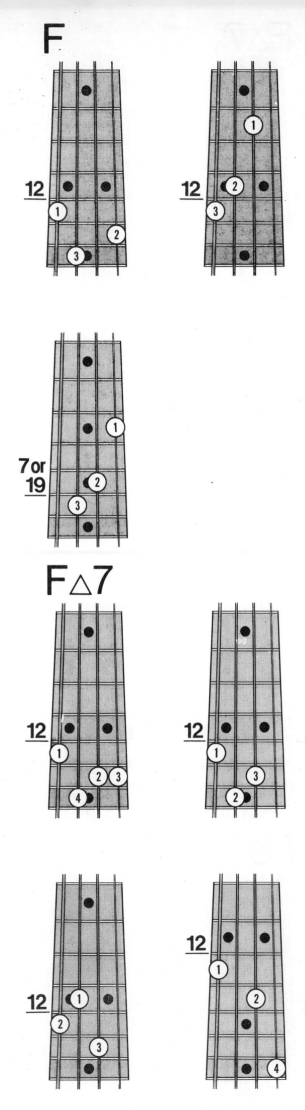

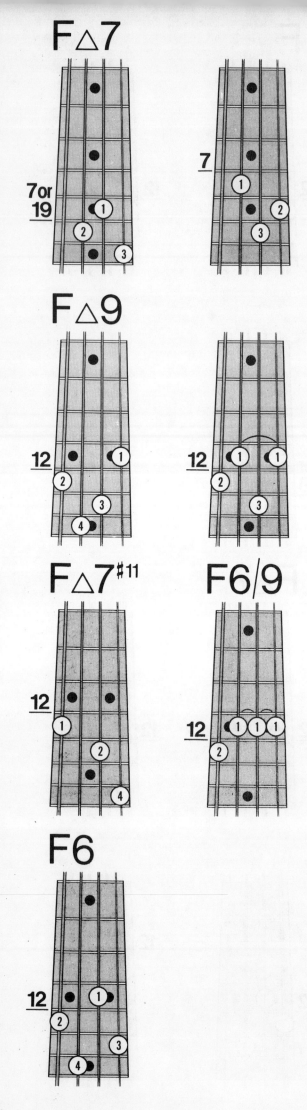

12

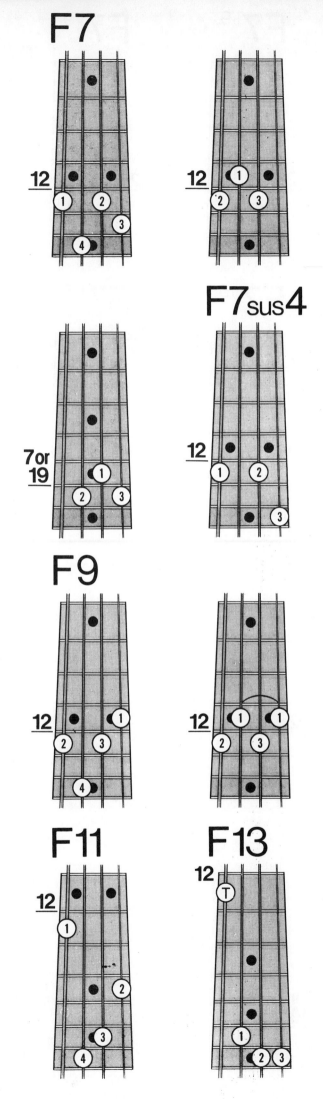

13

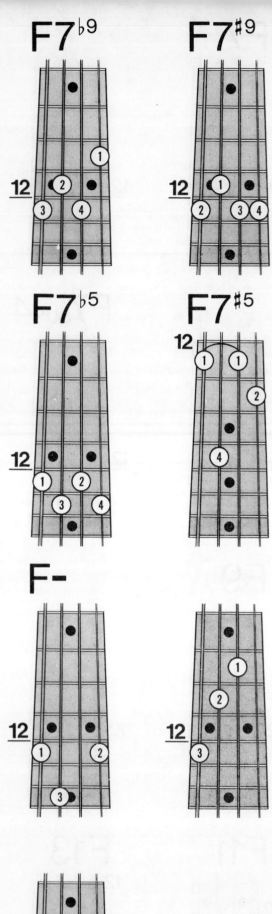

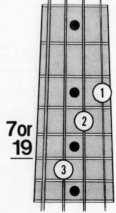

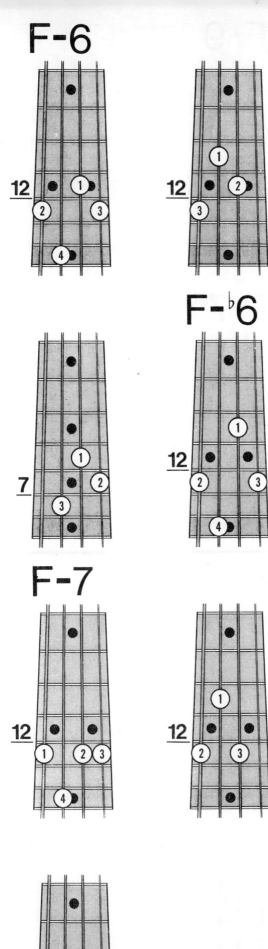

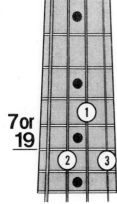

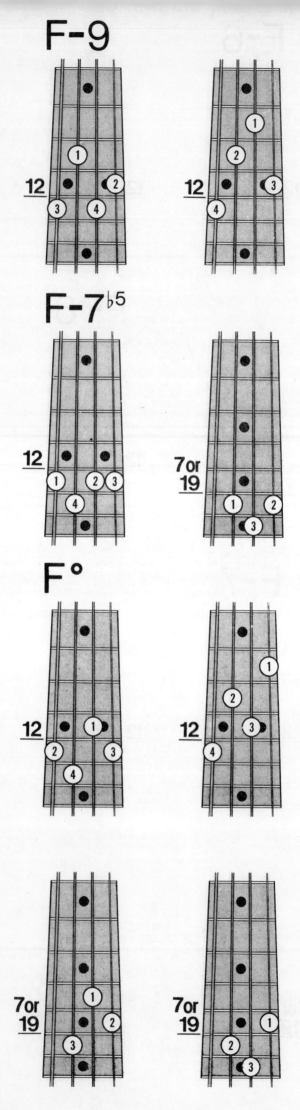

16

F#/G♭

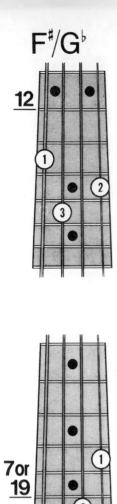
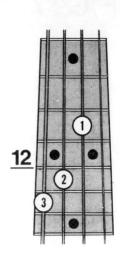
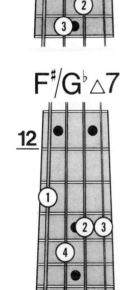

F#/G♭△7

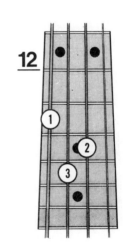
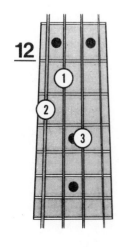
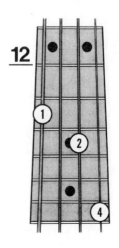

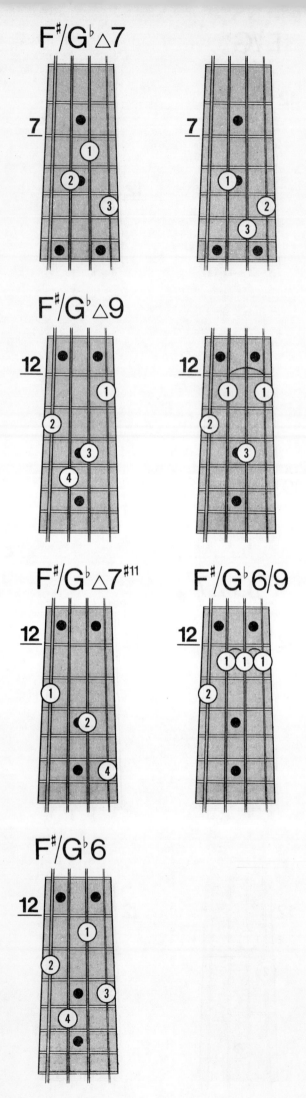

18

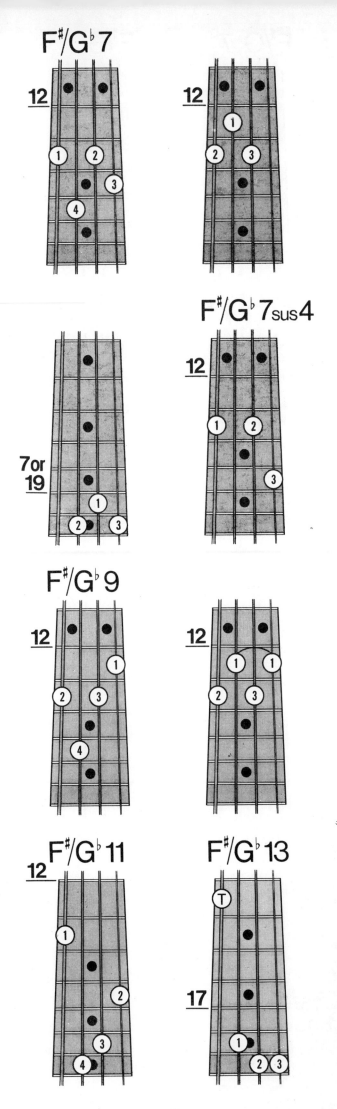

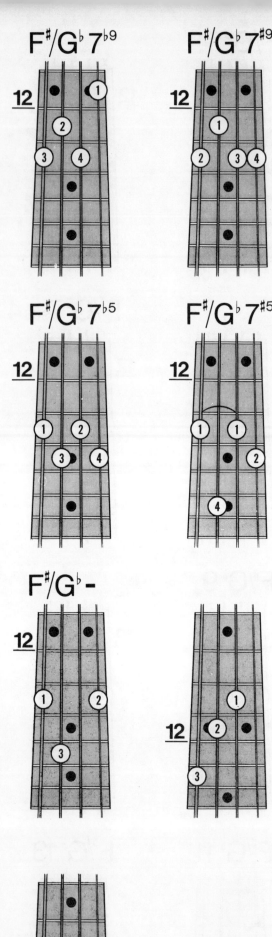
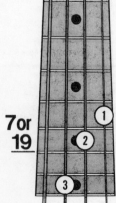

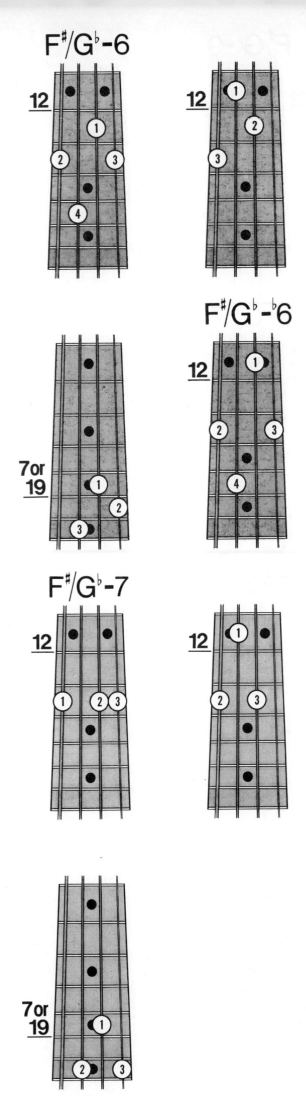

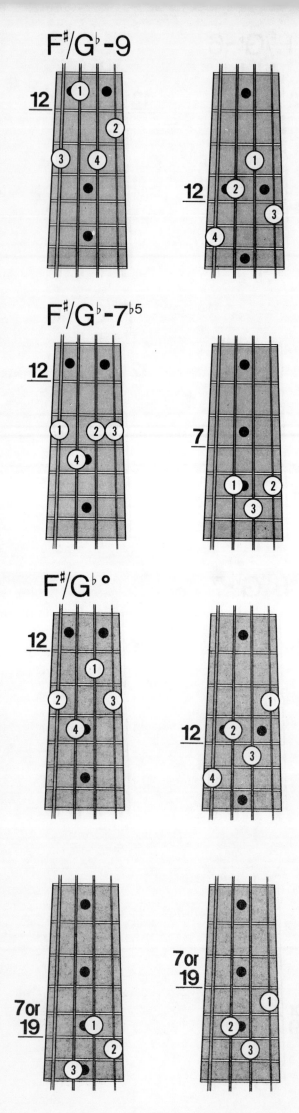

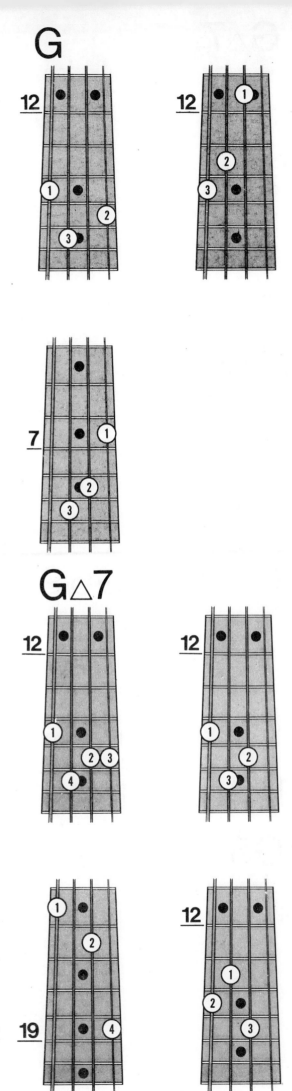

G

G△7

23

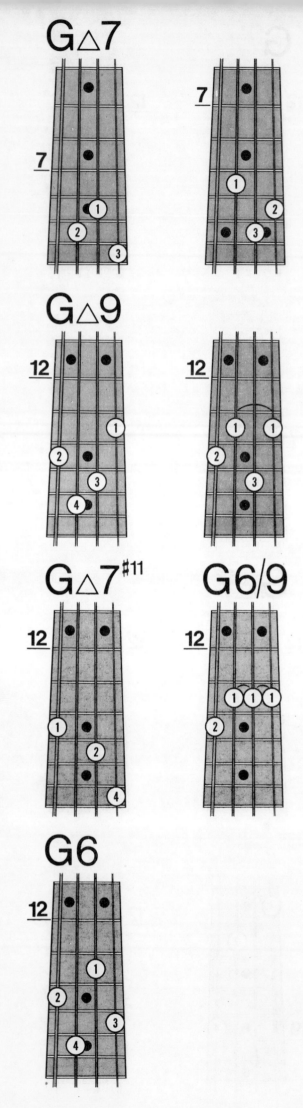

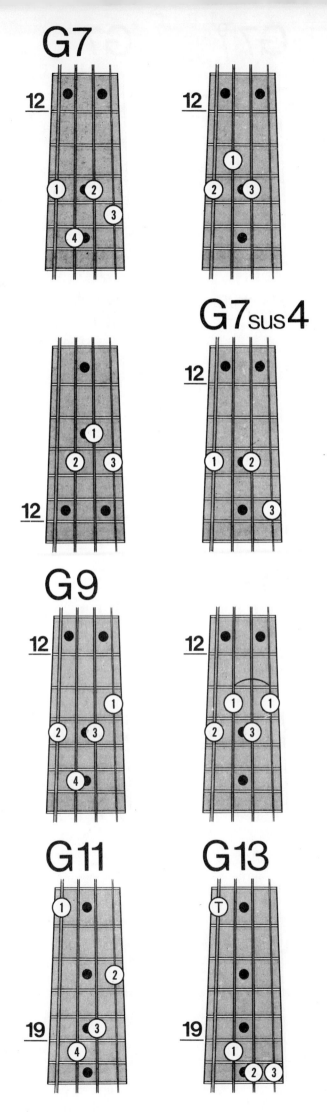

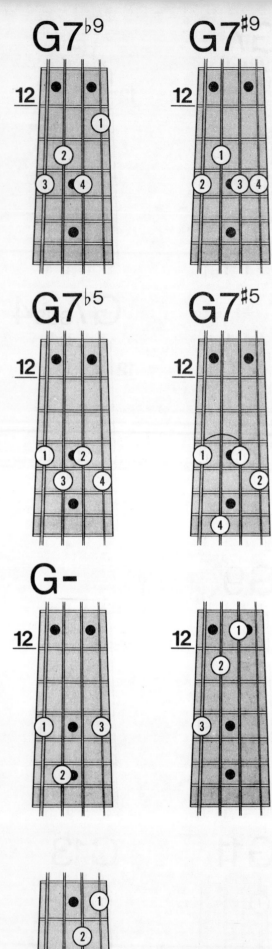

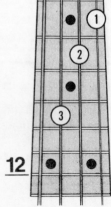

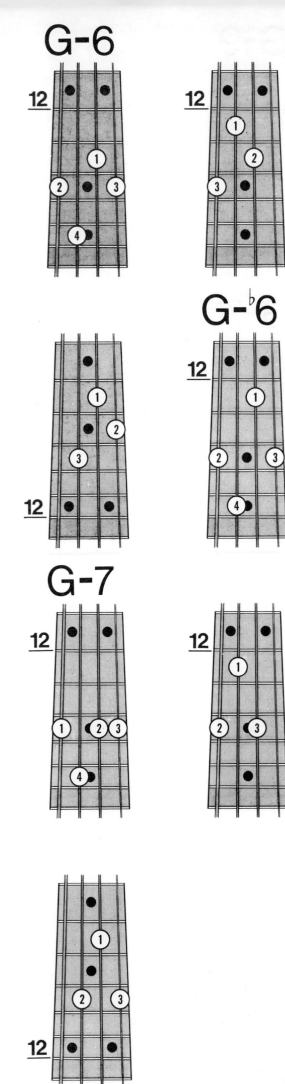

G-6

G-♭6

G-7

27

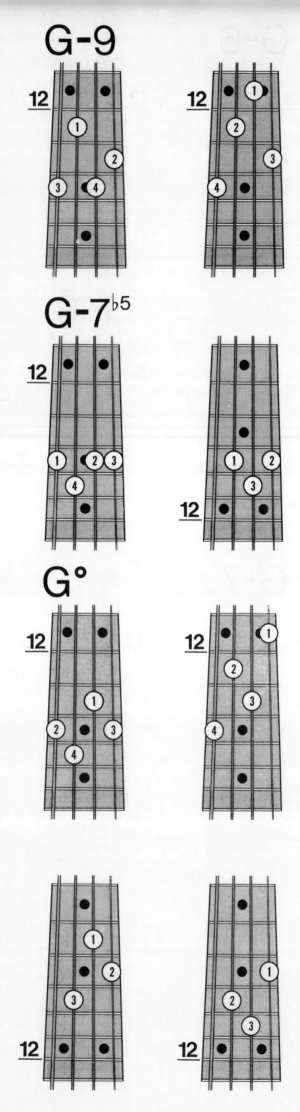

28

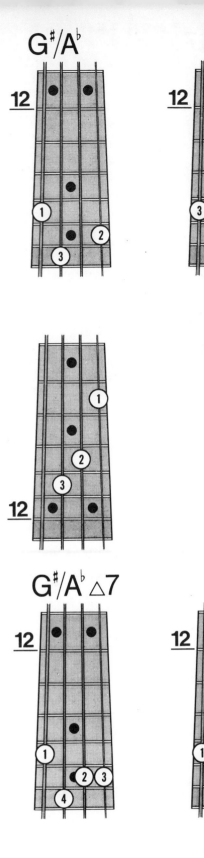

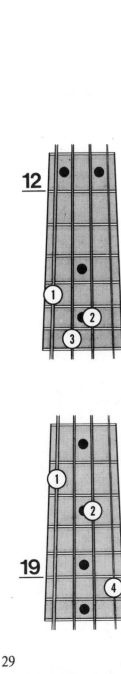

29

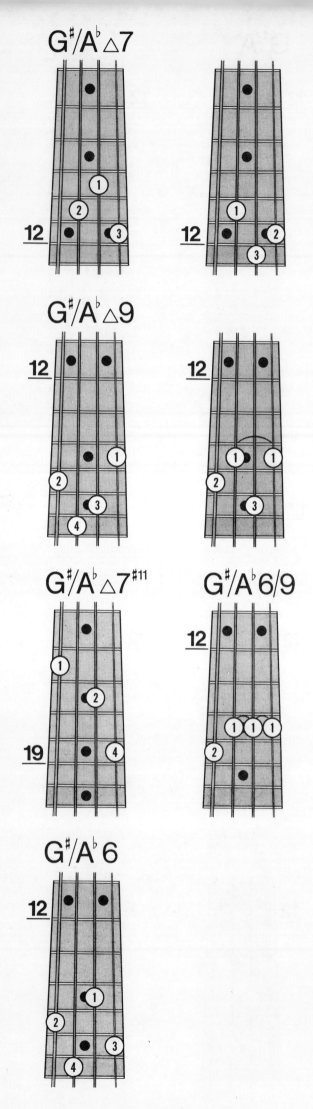

30

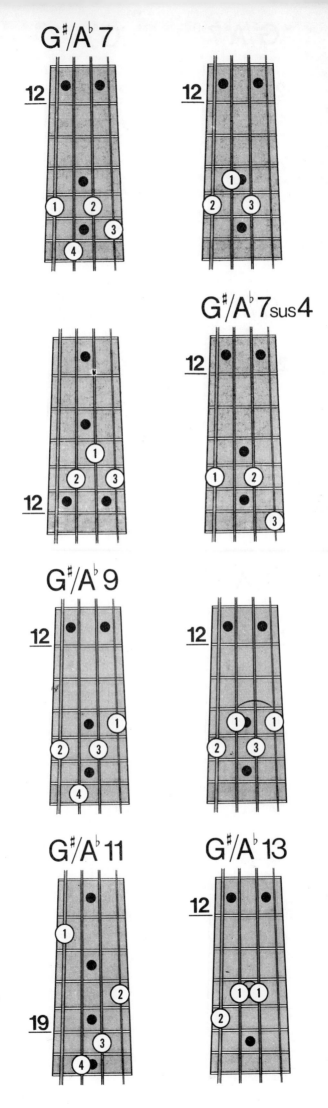

31

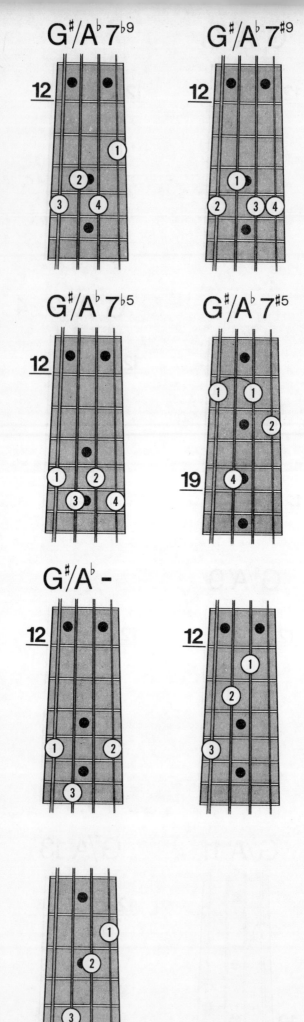

G#/A♭-6

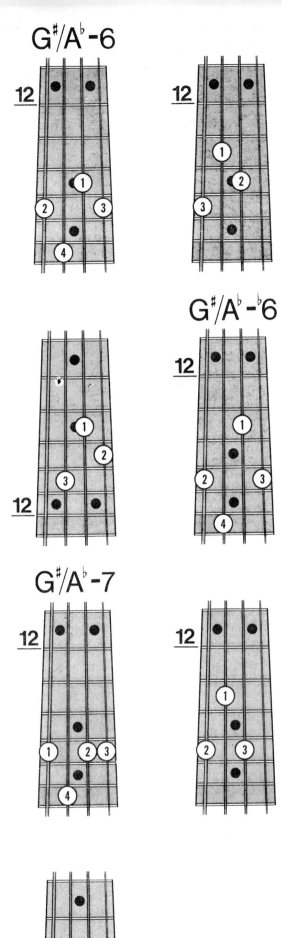

G#/A♭-♭6

G#/A♭-7

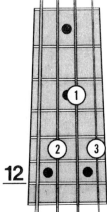

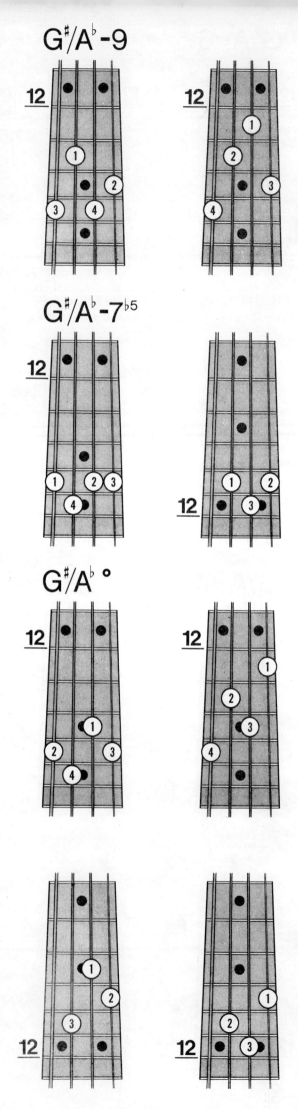

34

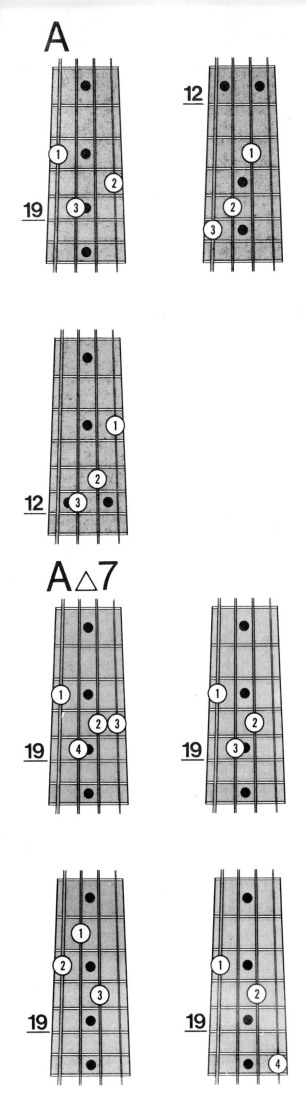

35

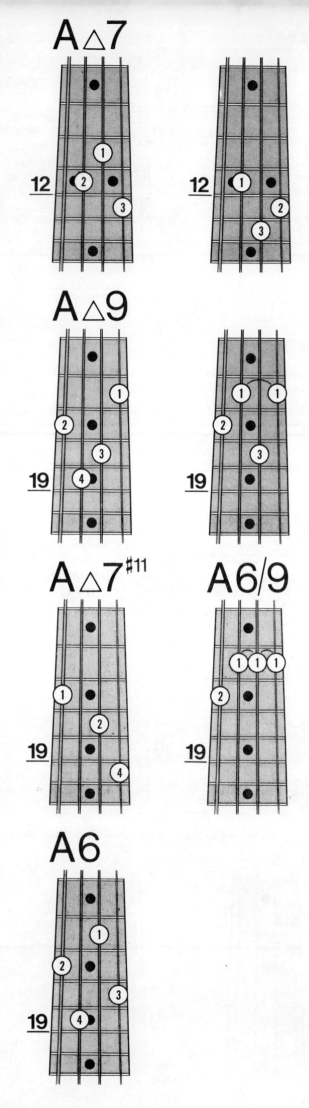

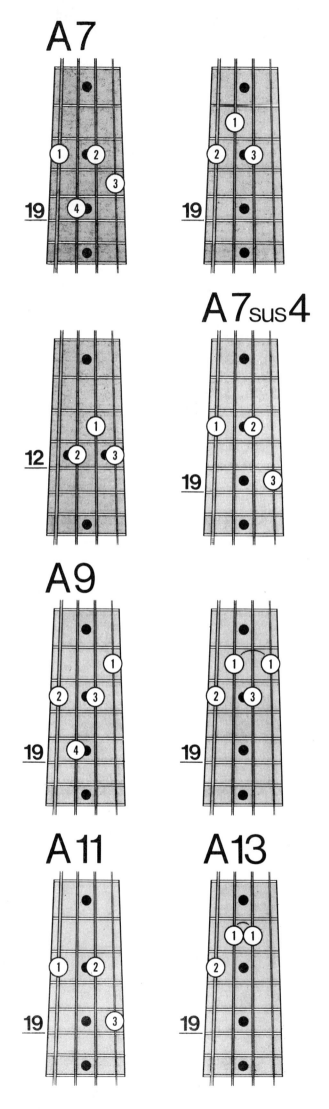

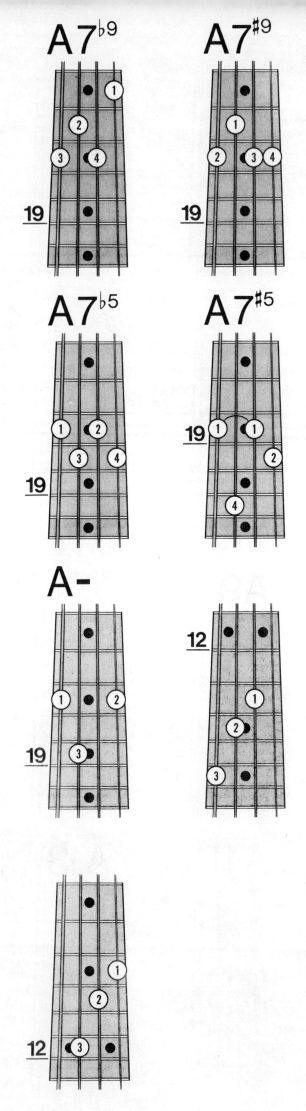

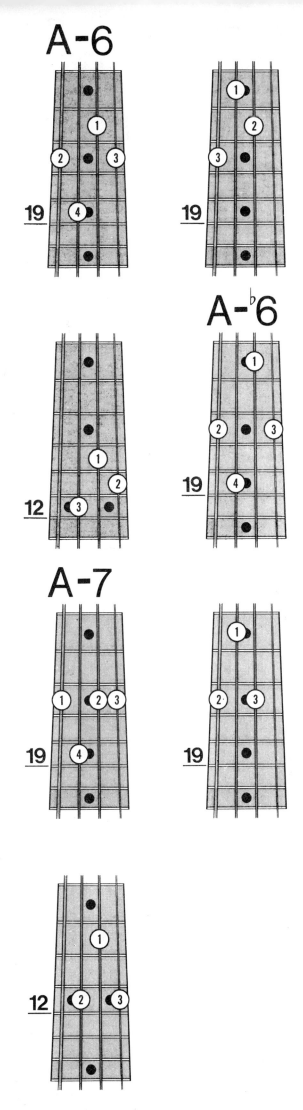

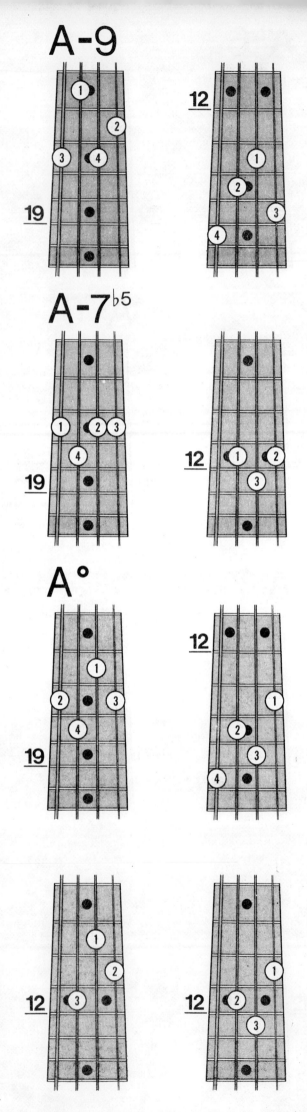

40

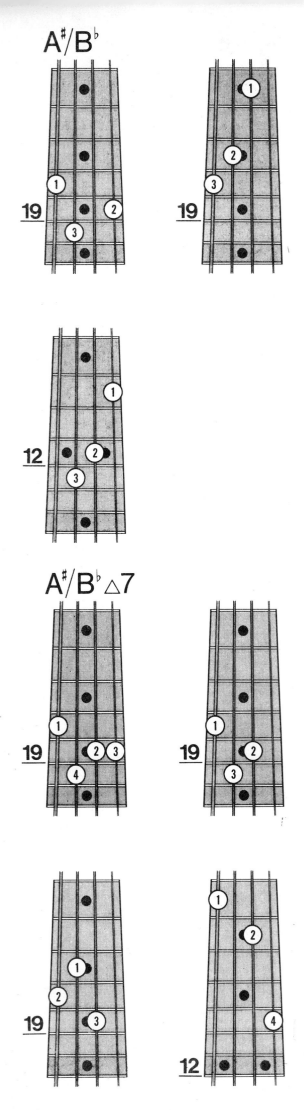

41

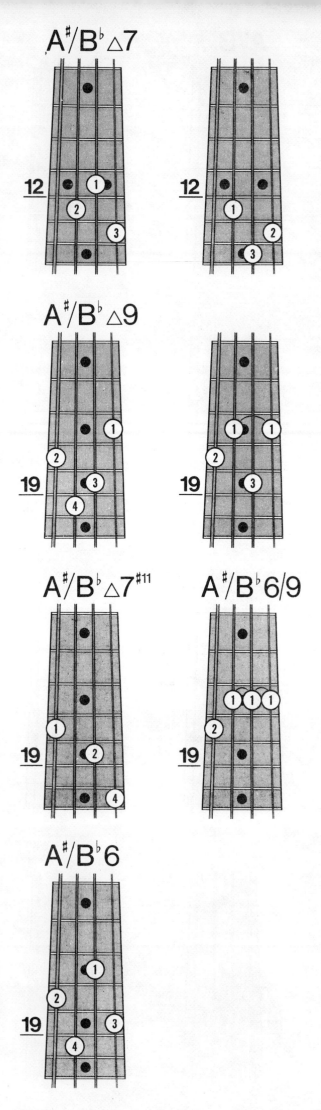

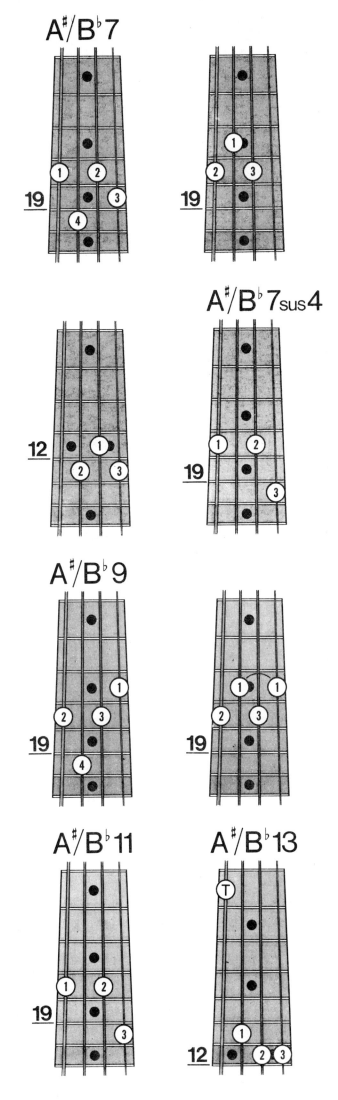

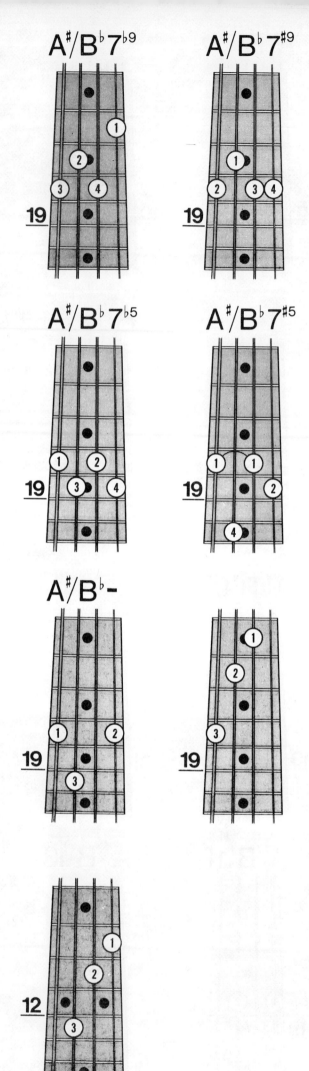

44

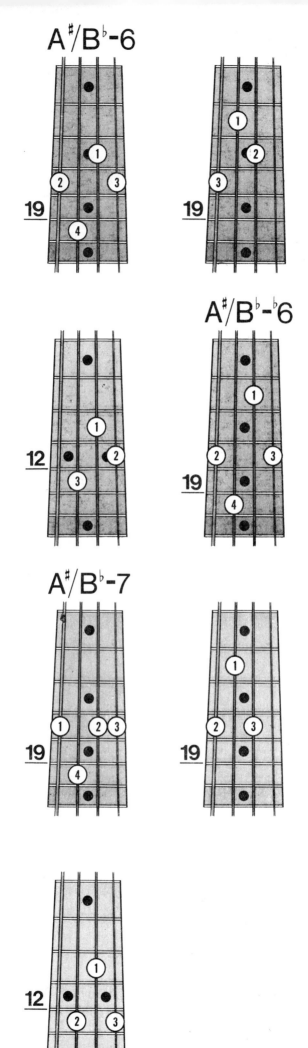

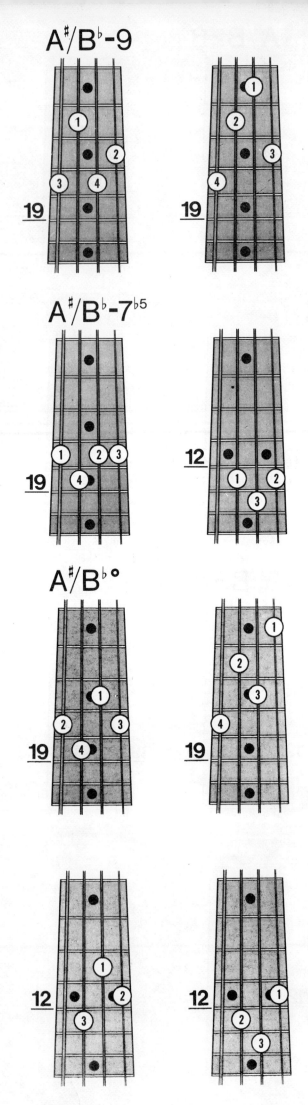

B

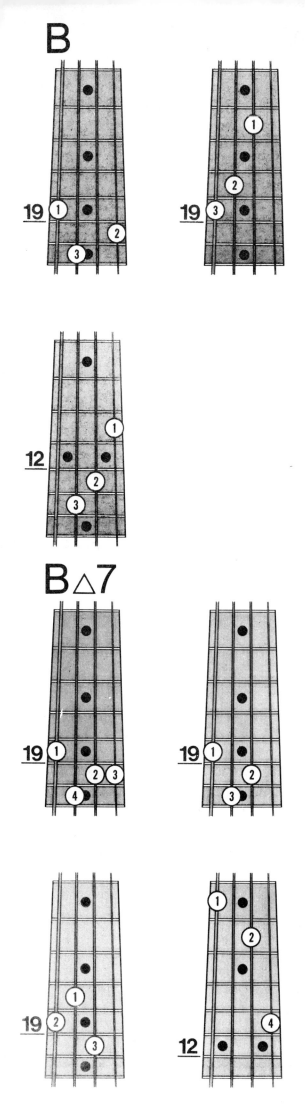

B△7

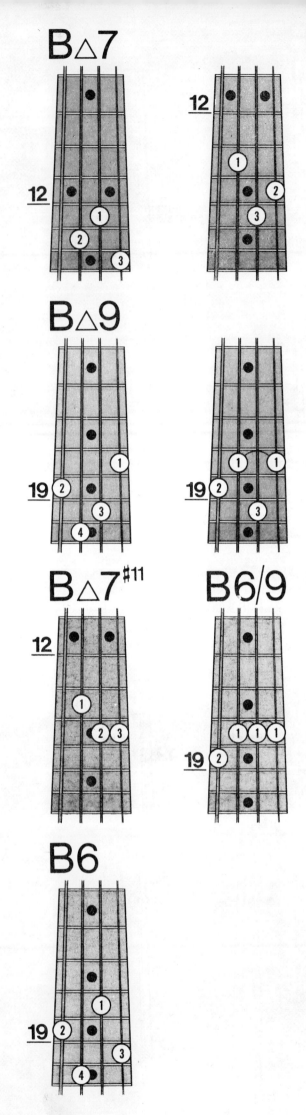

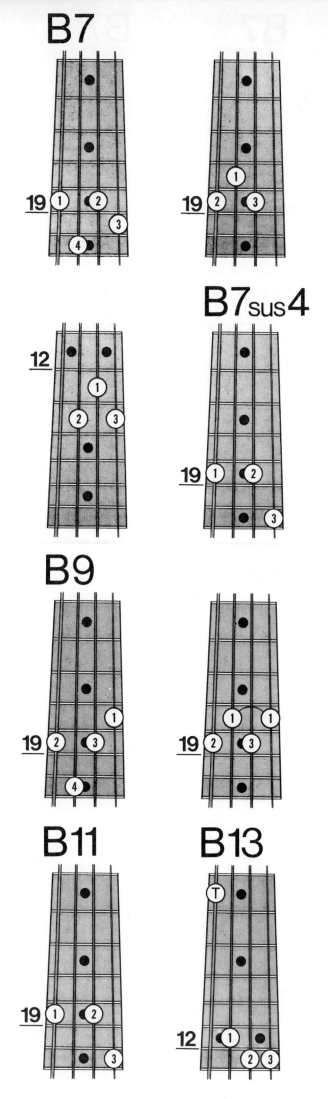

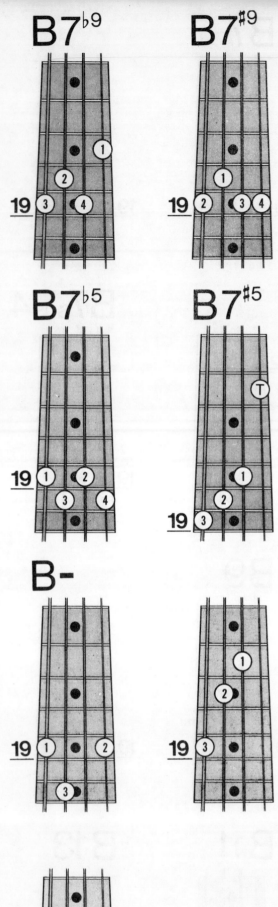

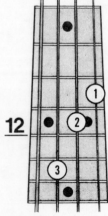

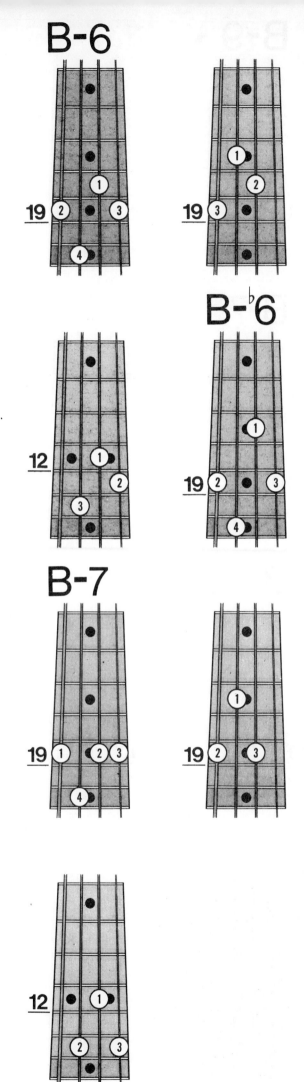

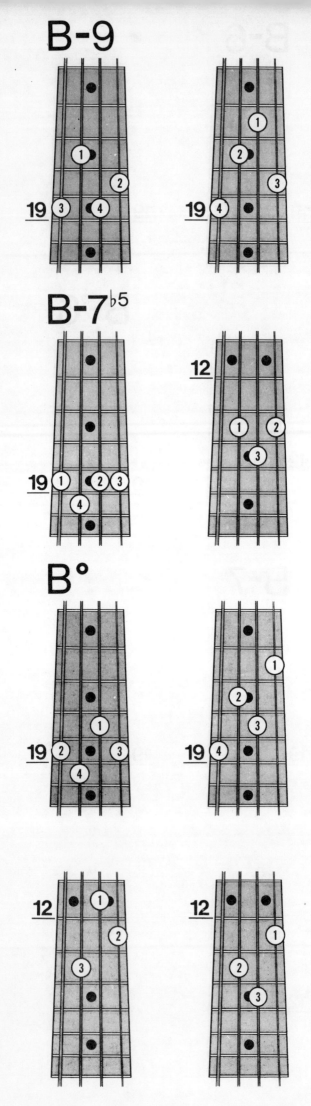

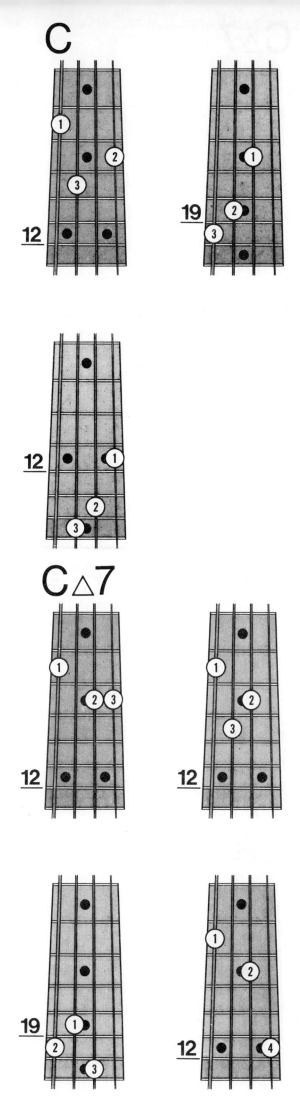

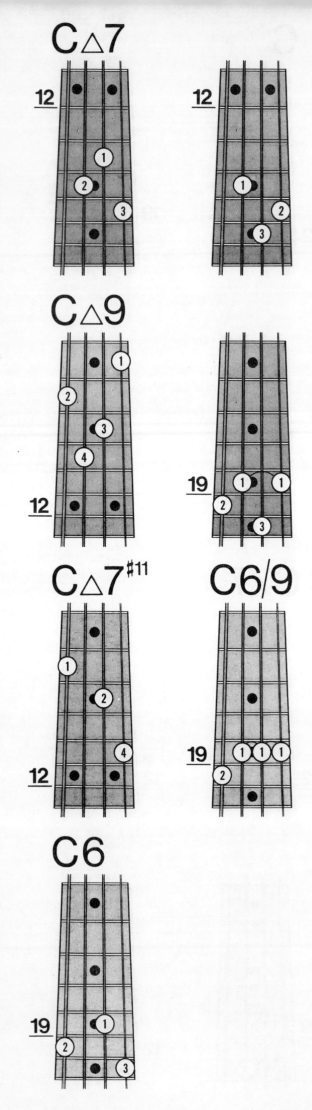

54

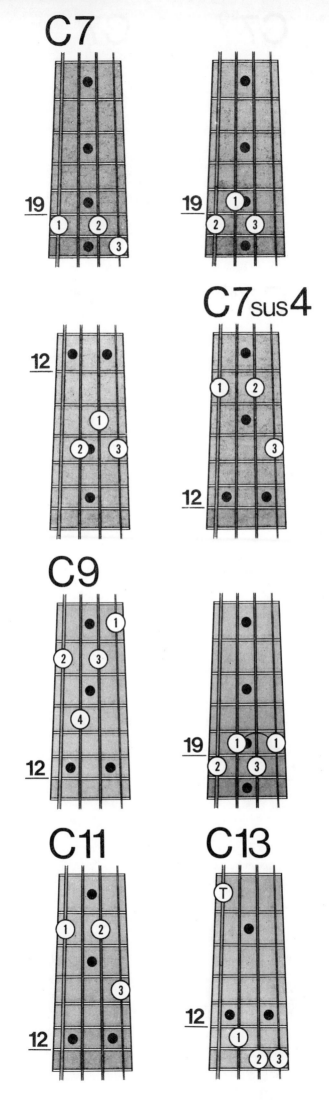

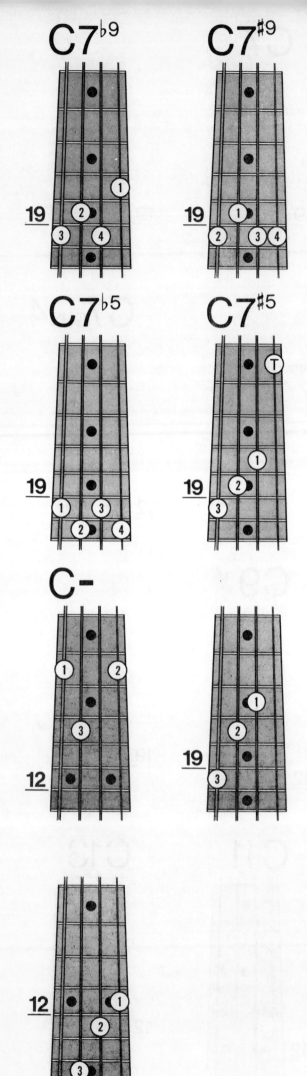

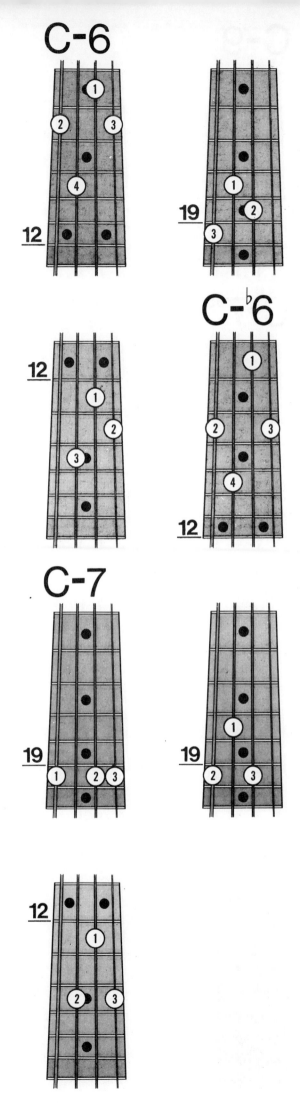

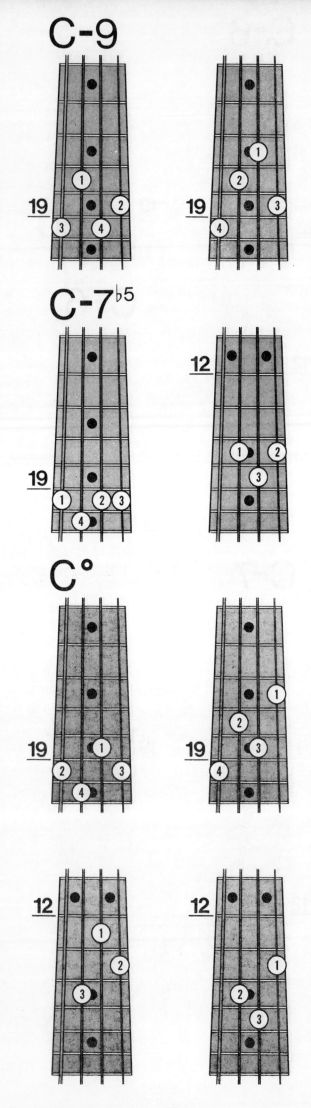

58

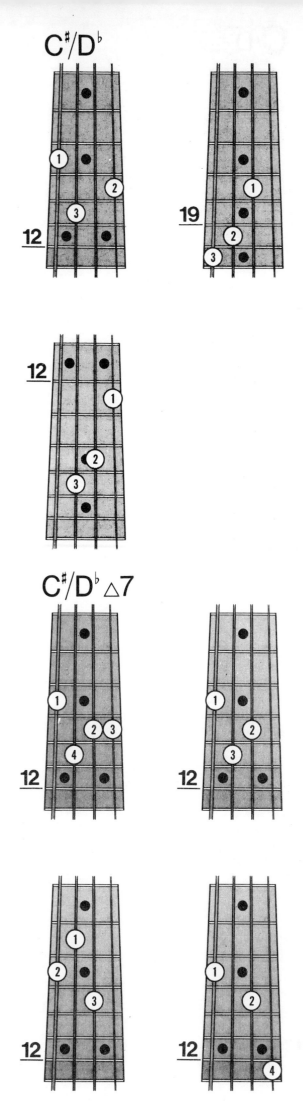

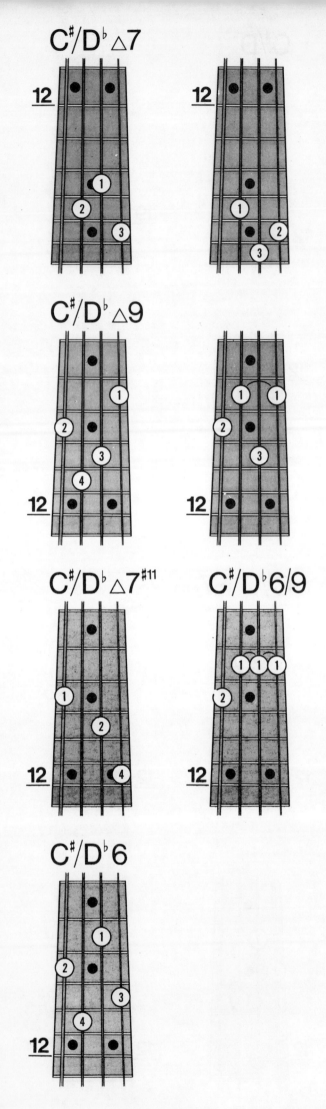

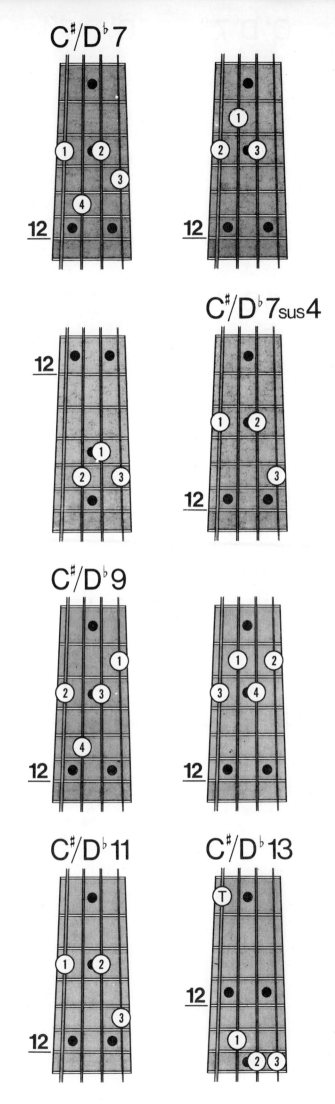

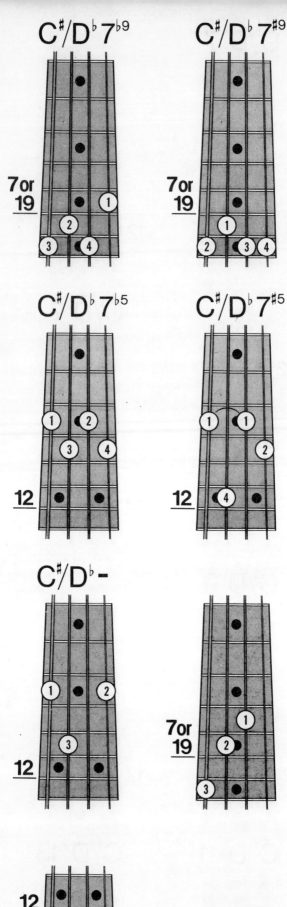

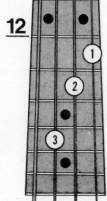

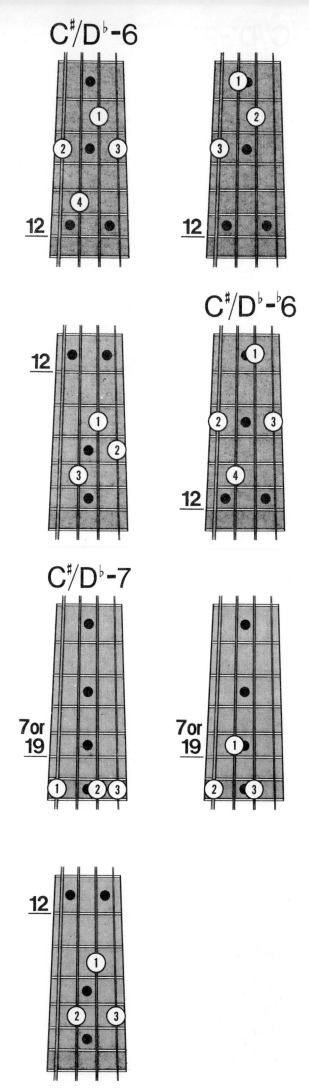

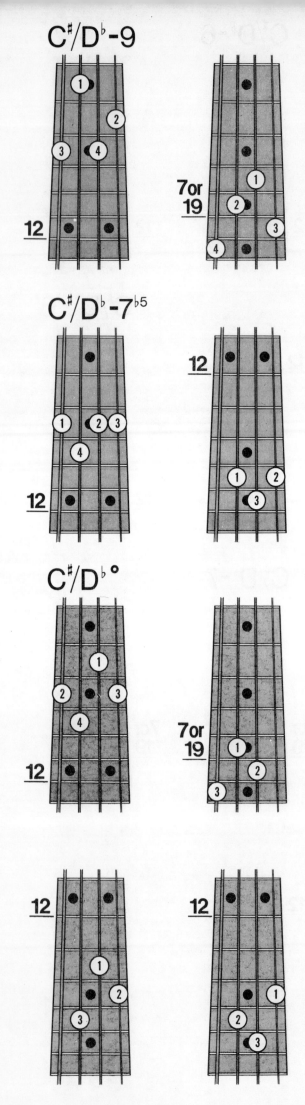

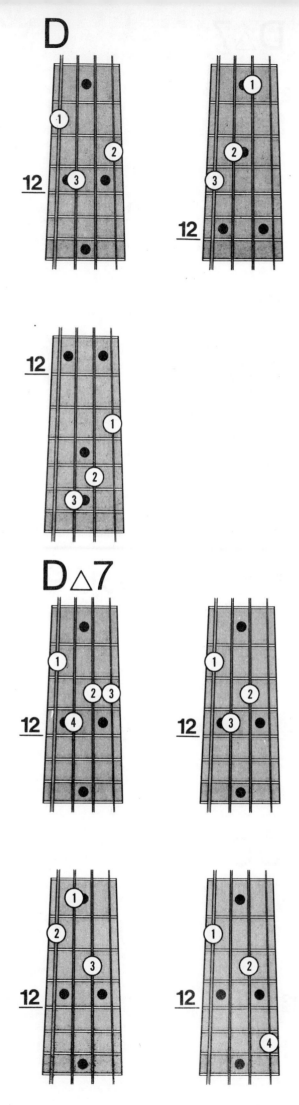

D

D△7

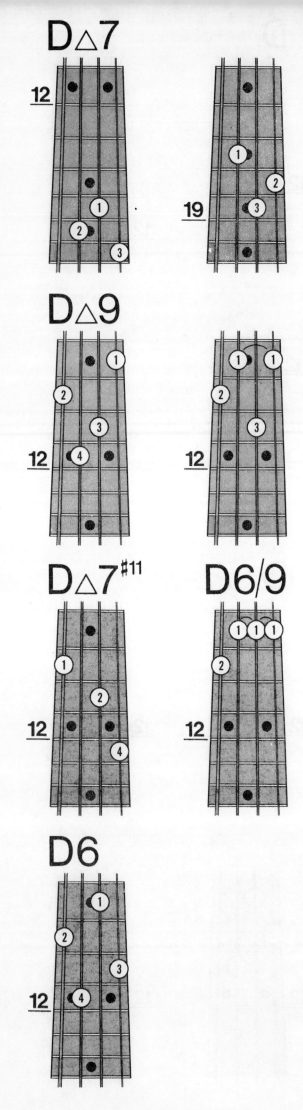

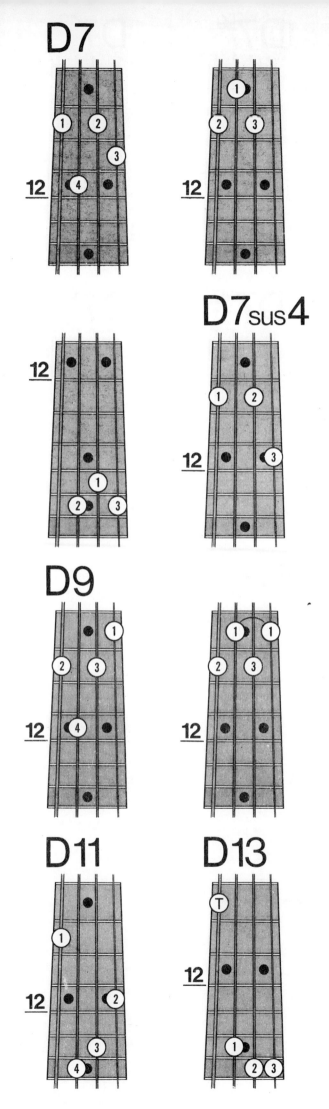

D7

D7sus4

D9

D11

D13

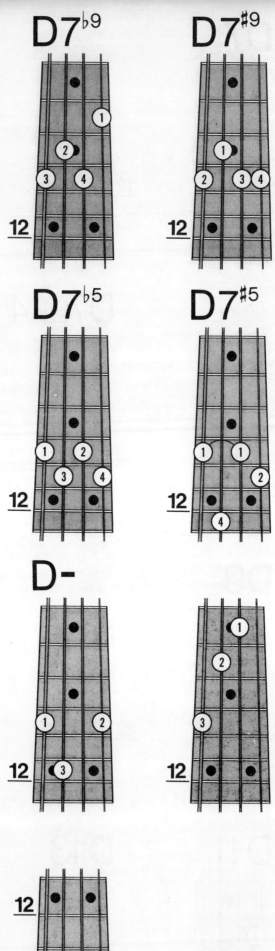

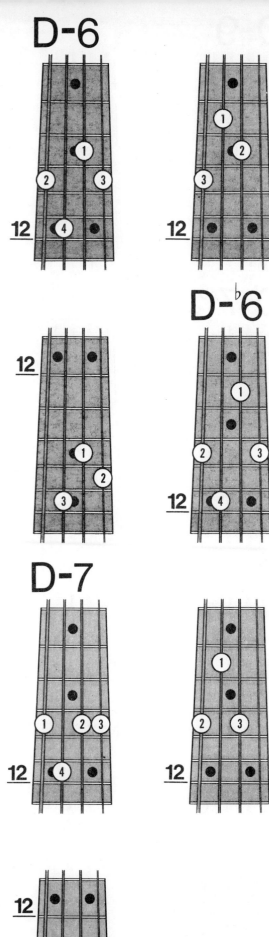

D-6

D-♭6

D-7

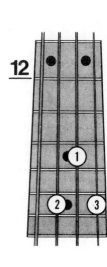

69

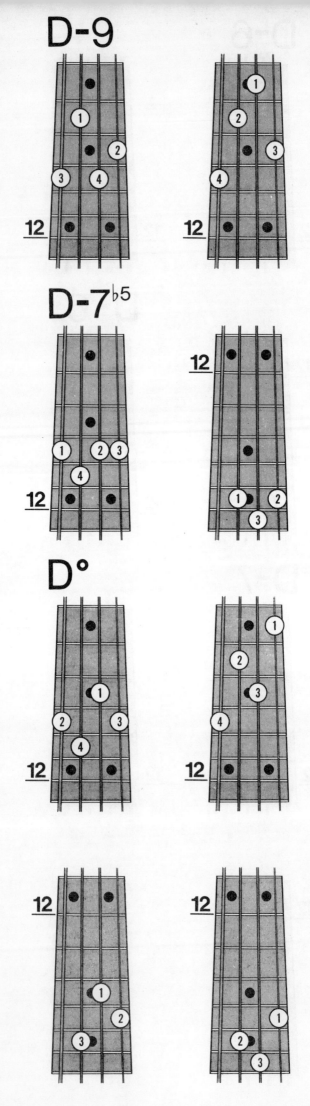

70

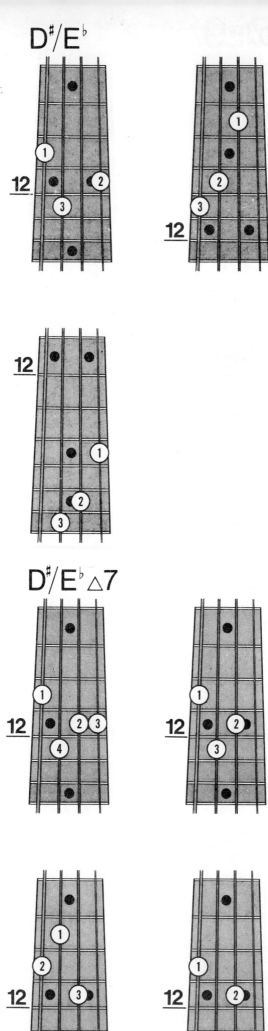

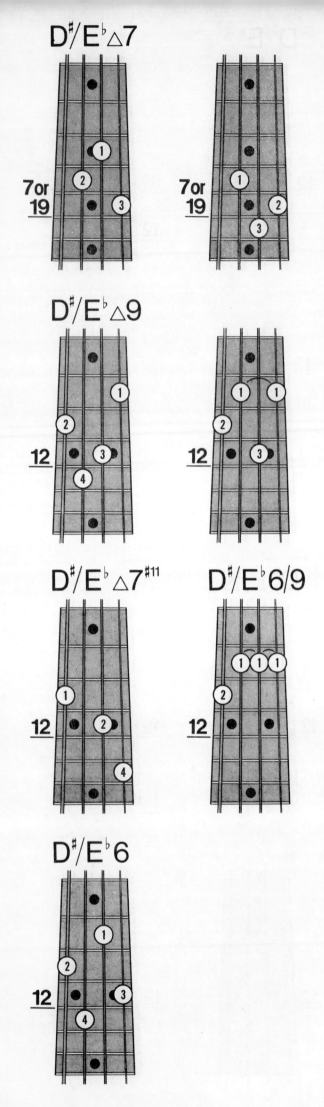

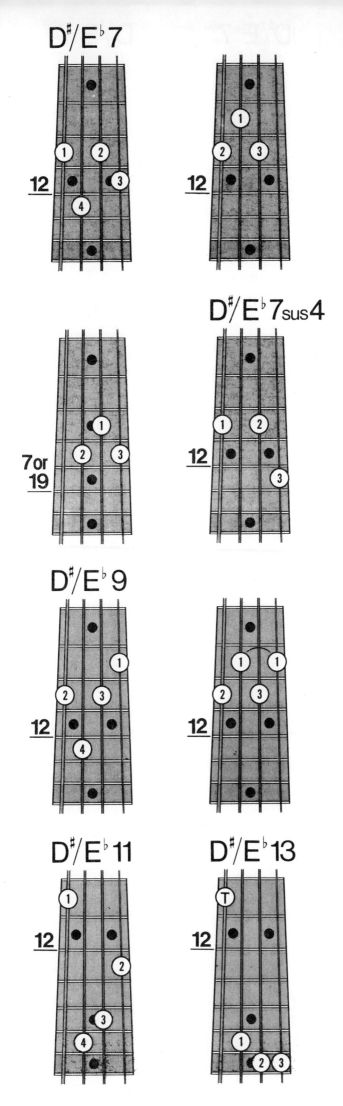

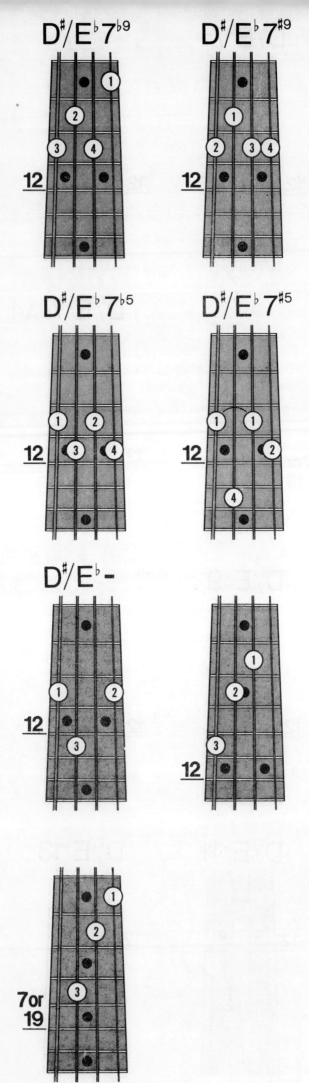

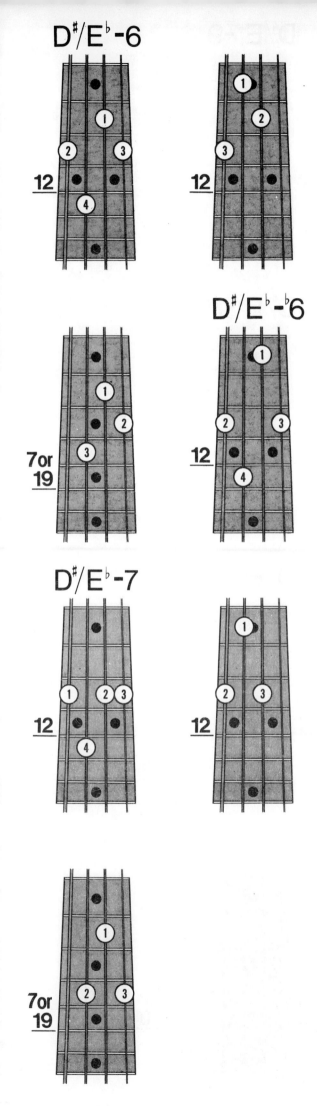

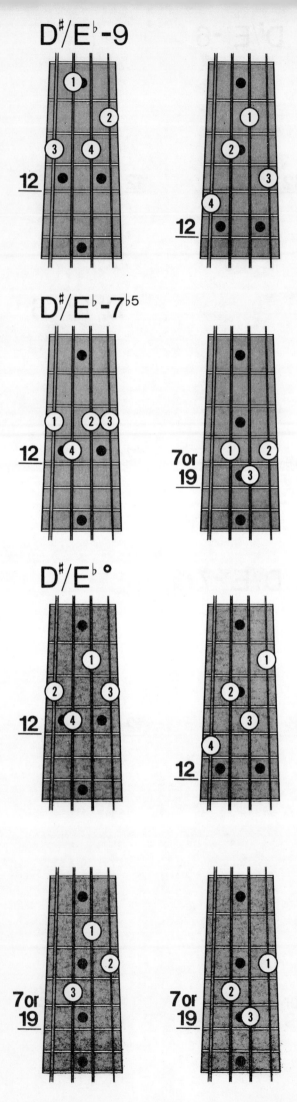